THE GHOST
IN THE CLOUD

BOB KILPATRICK

For my wife,
Cindy,
who dances with me
in the Cloud

the Ghost in the Cloud

©2018 Bob Kilpatrick
All rights reserved. International copyright secured.
This book is protected by the copyright laws of the United States of America. Copying any portion of this book without prior written permission, except for review or the use of short quotations, is expressly forbidden.

Additional copies of this book and other books by Bob Kilpatrick are available by visiting
bobkilpatrick.com
or by writing to
Bob Kilpatrick Ministries, Inc.
P. O. Box 2383
Fair Oaks, CA 95628
(discounts given on multiple copies)

Other books by Bob Kilpatrick
The Art of Being You
Secrets of the Silence
Sacred Synergy

cover design, Ian Kilpatrick
a PrayerCanvas book

Acknowledgements

Writers who influenced this book and me: Dorothy L. Sayers, Jean Pierre de Caussade, Leslie Newbiggin, GK Chesterton, CS Lewis, Michael Heiser and many others either too far in the past to remember how their thinking informed and strengthened me, or in snippets whose source is forgotten but whose impact is still felt.

Friends who enrich me through their lives, books and conversations: Cindy Kilpatrick, Bill & Beni Johnson, Manuel Luz, Chris Howard, James Alexander, Dr. Gene Maynard & Dr. Ron Harden (of Epic Bible College)

My family, with whom I have sweet fellowship and deep conversations about God:
Joel & Ana Maria, *Ian, Evan, Rachel, Kate & Jane*
Ian & Jennifer, *Reagan, Maxwell, Sam A, Lucy & Finn*
Andrew & Ashley, *Madeline, Chandler, Jackson, Elizabeth, Charles & Anne*

Kyle & Emily, *Adelaide, August Robert & Hazel*
Britt & Eric Howard, *Hudson, Hannah & Hamilton*

> I thank God for you all.

Foreword

There are so many reasons you could have to write a book: God told you to write a book; you have something you feel is important to communicate; you love words; you love your own way with words (similar to liking the sound of your own voice); you want others to think more highly of you; you want them to buy your book. This is not a comprehensive list but it touches the high points. I wish I were humble enough to say that only the first two were in my mind, but who knows their own heart?

I do know this: I could not have written this book ten or twenty years ago, perhaps not even five years ago, because I was too concerned how people might react to some of the ideas and experiences I share in it. Happily, I did not die yet and have now lived to an age when I do not much care anymore what naysayers might make of this book.

I *do* love words and I *do* love a well turned phrase. I've had a lot of joy and pleasure writing books and songs. This is different. There is an experience of God for which there is no language. Paul mentions this. The phrase *"words cannot contain"* comes to mind. Nonetheless, I wanted to try to describe a way of knowing Him that would enrich your life with Him.

And so I wrote this book.

CHAPTER 1

"You are happy with the map while I offer you the terrain."— Jean Pierre de Caussade

Words are important. They are the way we communicate thoughts and meanings. But we must be careful to realize that a word is not the thing itself. Words are metaphors. They represent a thought or an image, but they are not that thing. In 1929 Rene Magritte showed his famous painting "The Treachery of Images" in which he painted a pipe with the French sentence "Ceci n'est pas une pipe." underneath it. (In English- "This is not a pipe.") The image of the pipe is not a pipe. It is a representation of a pipe. You cannot fill it, you cannot light it, you cannot smoke it. What he was saying about images is also true of words. They are representations of something else. Words become images or stories in our minds and it is there where their meaning and effect is.

Words become the frame of our experience, and the images created by them delimit our expectations.

As an example, let's take the statement *"I am a follower of Christ"* and examine what images are made from it. The first image is created by the word "I." The follower is alone in this action. This is a solitary endeavor. It does not say *"We are followers of Christ."* This would seem to indicate, and could make you believe, that a relationship with Christ is only personal and that you can successfully do it without others. This is, of course, not a scriptural idea but it is certainly pervasive in Western and, particularly, American thinking. Americans strongly emphasize individuality over communality. So, in our mental image, one is alone with Christ. This is the first delimitation or de-scription of our expectations created from the image made by the words.

The second strong idea in this sentence is that of being a follower. To be a follower one should be behind the leader, both facing the same direction. Following indicates movement. So, the follower is moving behind the leader, maintains a suitable distance, doesn't fall behind and doesn't veer off the path the leader takes. However, the image of a leader and a follower doesn't lend itself to conversation or relationship. In all probability, the leader is looking away from the follower in your mental image. As a friend of mine put it, the goal of the follower is to 'keep up and shut up.' This second part of the vision created by the words further establishes the border around what we can expect from 'following' Christ. We can certainly be with Him, as a soldier is with his commander or as a hiker is with a guide, but it's not very convivial.

There is a stronger image given in the Bible in which the Holy Spirit is called our Paraclete, or the one called alongside. 'Alongside' is very different than following, isn't it? It creates an entirely different image and, consequently, an entirely different expectation. In another place Jesus tells us to take His yoke upon us. Like oxen yoked together, He asks us to go side by side with

Him. But so many Christians think of themselves as only followers and never come alongside Jesus because the story they tell themselves — *I am a follower of Christ* — doesn't lead them to envision anything different.

Now, let's take another saying; a well known one many of us have incorporated into our lives.

What Would Jesus Do?

This little question made its appearance first in a book (*In His Steps*, by Charles Sheldon), then on wristbands (WWJD), in songs and posters and T-shirts and seemingly every other medium in which an idea could be represented and exchanged. It's a pithy and, on the surface, attractive little saying. It encourages us in the prevailing purpose Christians seem to have these days — to be *like* Jesus — but the underlying presumption is a dangerous one.

The question presumes that Jesus is not here.

You would have no reason to ask such a question in the third person if you believed that Jesus were actually alive and present. Jesus says that He will never leave us or forsake us. He tells us that He will be with us always. (both in John 14) Do you believe Him? Elsewhere, the Bible says that in Him all things consist (Col. 1:17) and that He holds all things together by the word of His power (Heb. 1:3). Do you believe these verses? The Bible is very clear on these points: God is alive: God is present: God is relational. Some Christians believe that at some point — the death of the last of the twelve or thirteen or fourteen apostles, or the completion of the last of the treatises that would become the Bible — all mystical and supernatural occurrences ceased (that's why it's called Cessationism) and, presumably and inexplicably, Jesus chose to go silent and communicate only through what has come to be called the Written Word. This is not only biblically indefensible and plain wrong, it is also, more importantly, against the nature of the Living God. *"In the beginning was the Word, and the Word was with God and the Word was God."* (Jn. 1:1)

It does not say that in the beginning was the Vision, Taste or Touch. God is called the Word because He is a communicative being and He is alive. (John is referring here to Jesus, not the Bible.)

The letters we use to visually form words are representative of sounds we make when we speak. We arrange the letter-sounds into written words that mimic on the page the words we say. The spoken language came first, then the written counterpart. One is derivative of the other. In other words, the written language is the child of the spoken language. Let me say it another way. The written Word is the child of the spoken Word.

A word that is spoken must come from a living being. Dead people do not speak. Inanimate objects do not speak. It is when a living being expresses a thought vocally that a word is spoken. Even in this act the word has become something else: it has become a vibration — a wave, a rhythm — moving through the air. The written word, on the other hand, is a recollection of something. It is secondary. It is the memory or account of an act of a living being. In the case of the Bible, it is an accurate and true representation of who God is. As the Westminster Confession of Faith states, *"The Bible, uniquely and fully inspired by the Holy Spirit, is the supreme and final authority on all matters on which it speaks."* The Bible becomes our touchstone to try all revelations to ensure that what we are hearing resonates with the character of God. He will never speak contrary to His own nature. He is one. In Him there is no shadow of turning, no flicker of change. He is holy — full and complete in Himself, lacking nothing. His nature revealed in the Bible is His true nature. Therefore, we compare and test what we believe we hear from His ever-present Ghost to what the Bible says of Him to see His nature and character truthfully and harmoniously expressed. The Living Word and the written Word will never be in disunity. Though the written Word is our touchstone it nonetheless derives its power from the Living Word, not the other way round. They both faithfully witness of the other but it is the Living Word that is the superior because the Living Word is a person.

CHAPTER 2

For the first three hundred or so years of church history Christians had no Bible. Think about it: there was no such thing as a "Bible believing Christian" for centuries. They had the "memoirs of the Apostles" (which we call the four Gospels) and they had many other letters from Christian leaders circulating among the gatherings in various cities and towns, but none of these were universally accepted as divinely inspired and canonical. That took some time.

What did the early Christians have that made their faith so powerful that it overcame persecution and revulsion to profoundly change the known world at its very center of power? I have heard it said that they had an event — the resurrection — that they could remember. However, to say that the resurrection as an event, and the memory of it, is what powered them is to miss the power of the resurrection itself. Jesus rose from the dead! It was a person that was resurrected. The event is good but the presence of the resurrected person of God — forever alive and always present — is what really fueled the early Church. It wasn't a memory of a past event that gave them power, it was the constant, moment by moment presence of the Ghost of God — God Himself — that quickened them and made them alive.

More than being *"Bible believing Christians"* the early Church of God were *"Jesus believing Christians."*

I have an alternative question I would like to suggest that you make a habit of asking: *"Jesus, what are You doing?"* Then ask if you can do it with Him. Since the Bible calls Jesus the Divine Yes, I believe that that is how He'll answer — *"Yes! Come with me and let's do this together."* You were made for His presence, more than for His laws, principles or guidelines. As Paul says in 2 Corinthians 3, we were made to live with the Ghost of God, not just the writings of God. This is our calling. Instead of trying to be *like* Jesus, endeavor to be *with* Him. Trying to be like Jesus is a sure way to disappointment and discouragement. If you have tried, as I have, to live up to His example then you, like me, have known despair. It's not possible. Why not give it up? Living *with* Jesus is the sure way to peace and contentment. And the wonderful secret is that if you will be *with* Him, you will be *like* Him. You don't get God's character by pursuing *it*, you get it by pursuing *Him*.

John chapters 14-17 record Jesus preparing His disciples for life after the Ascension. Contrary to much popular interpretation, He does not deal here with the afterlife, as in heaven, but with the *"after I am gone from this body"* post-Ascension life. I have heard sermons and songs about mansions in heaven and Jesus going there to prepare a place for us. This interpretation doesn't fit the tenor of the rest of what Jesus talked about in these chapters. What leads to a misunderstanding of the oft-quoted *"In My Father's house are many mansions"* is the use of the word mansion by the King James translators. In our modern English we would not expect to find mansions inside a house but that's what a contemporary reading would infer. (And once again we see the power of images through words.) The Greek helps us to understand what Jesus is really saying. First, He refers to 'house' (Greek — *Oikia*) in the same way the Bible earlier talks about Joshua's 'house' serving God. (Joshua 24:15) It is not referring to the building where he lived but to the people who lived under his leadership. We could better read it "as for me and my family and staff…"

The word 'mansion' here is the Greek word '*mone*.' It first means 'a staying' and then, by inference, a 'residence.' I find it interesting that the first meaning of this word is a concept, not an object. A 'staying' is not the same as a residence. It seems to be more a *way* to be rather than a *place* to be. But by tying this idea of a residence to the statement that Jesus is going to prepare a place for us, we tend to see this as a place we are to go to some time in the future. We believe it's as though Jesus was saying that He was going to heaven and readying the place for us and then would come back (the

Second Coming) and take us there. This is the popular version. It is my belief, though, that Jesus was talking about the cross when He referred to going to prepare a place for us. Let me give you Kilpatrick's version:

"In My Father's family there are many stayings, or placements. If it weren't so I would have told you. I'm going to the cross to prepare a perfect spot (Gr. — topos*) for you."*

The work of the cross makes it possible for you to take your place in God's family. Think of it as the mosaic of the community of God and the spot He has made for you in it. Or think of it as the Body, including the eyes, ears and all the other parts that contribute to wholeness. The message is that there is a place for you in God. There is a spot where you fit and all the joy and contentment you were made for can be found there.

The word *mone* is only used twice in the Bible and both in this same chapter. In the first (mansion) we are given the idea that we will move from where we are to another spot to which God will take us. We move. We interpret it to mean that our *mone* is in heaven, in eternity, but not here. The second and only other time the word is used, however, gives a completely different picture. In verse 23 Jesus says, speaking of Himself, the Father and the Ghost, that *"... We will come to him and make Our home* (mone) *with him."* In this verse the movement is all on God's side —

"...We will come..."

God's desire is to make His 'staying' with you in your present circumstance. In other words, the *mone* that Jesus has prepared for you is not a 'by-and-by' eventuality but a present moment reality. This moment, right now, is your moment to live in God. There is so much richness in this word *mone*, 'staying.' It speaks of abiding; of entering into the rest of God; of finding the still center; the unity with His rhythm; of constant companionship with Jesus; of being alongside Him; of finally finding our home in Him.

"Thou hast made us for thyself, and our heart is restless until it finds its rest in thee."— Augustine, Confessions

CHAPTER 3

Language changes over time. We don't use the word *wist* for *knew* like the King James Version translated Paul — "I wist not, brethren.…" (Acts 23:5) To my dismay, the non-words *integrous* and *impactful* continue to encroach on our sensibilities and will soon be acceptable usage. That's what happens. People make up words, like little boats full of meaning, and set them floating in the stream of language. Then there are the words that we've heard and read before that take on another meaning than the original or intended one. We say we can *dig* it without thinking of a shovel or a hole. Musicians talk about *gigging* but so do people who eat frog legs. In the film The Princess Bride one character keeps saying *"I don't think that word means what you think it means."*

CS Lewis in the Chronicles of Narnia tells a tale of four children leaving England by way of a wardrobe in a spare room in the house of their caretaker professor to mysteriously appear in a wooded area by a street lamp in the land of Narnia. A short time later (in our world) they return to find that centuries have passed in Narnia and there has built up a myth and a language about them. In the myth they, the two kings and two queens of Narnia, came from the country of Spare Oom and the city of War Drobe. As one critic noted, this was a clever way for Lewis to point out that words are symbols. They stand for concepts and ideas and their meanings are subject to a mutual agreement between those who share a language.

We make contracts, agreements and covenants with words, not pictures, because we can define them and agree on their precise meaning. But words do change and sometimes, as in Narnia, they can be capitalized into meaninglessness, and changed so much that the original meaning is lost. This has happened to many of the words Christians are familiar with from the Bible. I wonder, do you know what the word *glory* means? How about *selah*? *Shekinah*? even *faith*?

When we only had two sons, and they were about six and three years old, Cindy was praying with them as they went to bed. Joel, the oldest, had a sudden pain in his chest and let out a yelp, then another. Cindy asked what was wrong and Joel replied that he had a pain in his heart. Ian, the three year old, said "maybe it's Jesus trying to beat His way out." His understanding of *heart* hadn't quite widened out enough.

Words have power. We might tend to think that words make things known, or make things clear, but it is simpler and more powerful than that.

Words Make Things.

This is why the writer of Hebrews describes creation this way — *"...the worlds were framed by the word of God."* (11:3) We might read this simply as "the worlds were framed by God," but the phrase '*the word of*' is not superfluous. It is included for the very good reason that the word, or the expression of an imagination, is necessary to the creative process, both of God and of humans. God said let there be light, and there was light. *God said... there was.* Word becomes substance or energy.

In another book, *The Creation Principle*, I go into detail about the process of creation as shown to us most clearly in the concept of the Trinity. You can also find this idea brilliantly laid out in *the Mind of the Maker* by Dorothy L. Sayers. However, I will give a short explanation of God's creative process here.

God creates through a three-fold process or expression. This process is shown to us in the Trinity- Holy Father, Holy Son and Holy Ghost.

The Father is the Imaginer —
"Let us make..."

Jesus, the Son of God, Word of God, is the Expression or Embodiment of the imagination —
"...and the Word became flesh..."

The Holy Ghost is the Substantiation or Energy of the Expression —
"He (the Spirit) shall make alive..."

God always creates through this process. It never changes. God the Father imagines. God the Word expresses. God the Ghost makes it a reality. The Word is central and necessary to the creative process. God never makes anything that wasn't first imagined and then expressed through a word. Everything you perceive was made this way. All creation, all authorities, all miracles were and are made this way.

You are made in His image. Part of what this means is that you make things the same way God does. The human creative process is exactly the same as Gods. Hebrews 11:3 again tells us something very important about this creative process — *"... so that the things which are seen were not made of things which are visible."* All creation moves from the invisible to the visible. Everything created begins in the invisible as an imagination or a creative idea. Every idea is then expressed, perfected and refined. (I didn't understand Hebrews 5:8 until I saw this truth — *"...though He was a son, yet He learned obedience by the things which He suffered."*) Only then is it made substantial and energized. Again, all creation proceeds from the invisible to the visible. (This is one of the subtexts of the book of Hebrews.)

You have the inestimable privilege of becoming a part of God's creative process by speaking the words that come from His imagination. When the Bible says that we have the mind of Christ (1 Cor. 2:16) it is referring to the privilege we have of listening in on the same imaginations of the Father that created worlds and animals and people. You imagine with the Father, and express His imaginations in and with the Son (the Word), and the Ghost of God makes it a reality.

This is why it is vital that you guard your imaginations because you want to clearly and completely imagine the things that God imagines. If you are cluttering your mind with sinful or superfluous things you are hampering your ability to imagine His imaginations. If you spend no time with Him you cannot expect to think His thoughts or express His imaginations. Your prayer time should include time to be silent so that you can let His thoughts, imaginations and dreams be poured into your being. I talk about this in my book, *Secrets of the Silence*.

I was in a circle of people praying for a woman who was scheduled for surgery the next day to fuse five vertebrae in her spine. She was in constant pain and had limited movement. Someone prayed one of those "if it be Thy will" kind of prayers for her. While they were praying something happened in me. I knew as a certainty that she was made to be healed in this moment. I asked to pray for her again but first I wanted to see her range of movement. With much pain she tried to touch her toes, getting her hands only to her thighs. Then we prayed again, this time expressing the imagination of God that she was whole. God instantly healed her and her full range of motion was restored. The next day the surgery was cancelled because the X-rays confirmed that she was whole.

God's imaginations expressed by us are made real — substantiated — not by us but by the Ghost of God. There is no sweat in faith; no striving, no effort or work on our part other than to express His imagination. Faith is not hoping for substance, or believing for evidence. Faith *is* substance. Faith *is* evidence. The labor, or work, on our part is only to enter into the rest of God; to abide in Him; to seek that still and quiet place of imagining with him or, as my friend Bill Johnson says, dreaming with God. The Father invites you into His dreams, His imaginations, and is waiting for you to express them and see His Spirit make them a reality.

Your words are the stepping stones of your future. What words you say about yourself and your future will likely come true. Someone has famously said that if you say you can or say you can't, you're right. When you speak, the words you say are laying down the path that you will follow. We will sometimes say 'Amen' to some negative word that was said about us — *"you can't do anything right," "you've got no sense," "you'll never amount to anything"* — and we'll pick up the theme and repeat it to ourselves about ourselves. What began as a bad story about us becomes our own story, and this can lead us on a downward spiral to despair and destruction. More often, though, it leads simply to mediocrity — a walk without exploring, sight without seeing, thinking without dreaming, never risking, not fully alive.

"The glory of God is man fully alive!" said Irenaeus.

"The Son of Man came enjoying life!" said Jesus. (Mt. 11:19, Philips)

When you say *'Amen'* you are saying *'So Be It.'* You are agreeing in the present moment but you are also casting the words into your future. In effect, you are saying not only *'this is true'* but *'let this become true.'* Amen is a powerful word. What you say "amen" to will become your life.

Similarly, the word 'confess' in the Greek means to 'say the same as.' When we confess Jesus we are saying the same thing as God— we *Amen* it*!* Let's restate that verse that tells us that confession is good for the soul to read *"Saying the same thing as God is good for the soul."*

Change the witness to whom you say 'Amen.' Say 'Amen' to what God says about you. Take up His story of you as your own. When someone asks how you're doing, don't complain or whine or equivocate in the least. Answer that you are doing great — *Excellent!* Tell them that this is the best day of your life. Why? Because you have been translated into the Beloved; because all your sins have been forgiven; because His mercy is far deeper than any evil you have done; because the Father has lavished His love on you by naming you among His children; because there is nothing that can separate you from His love; because no one can measure the depth or width or height of the love God has for you; because He is with you in this moment, closer than your very breath; because this day is the *only* day you have and how good it is depends not on your circumstance but on your attitude. I'm not for a moment suggesting that you lie to yourself that things aren't hard, that pain doesn't hurt, that sin doesn't wreck things, that choices don't have consequences. I am saying to you that there is joy to be found in everything and, if you look, you will see God in every moment. Stephen looked into heaven while he was being martyred and saw the glory of God (Acts 7:55). See what Stephen saw in *your* present circumstance!

God never leaves you or forsakes you. Search the Bible for what God says about you and say 'Amen' to that. Listen for His voice to you today and say 'Amen' to that. Make His story your story. Say the same thing as God. A large part of our difficulty is that we think of many things as facts when they are only a story told by someone. Most of what we know, even about ourselves, is not fact…
…not truth…
…but story.

CHAPTER 4

Who are you? When asked this we generally start with the easiest and most flattering answer. We tell about what we do for work, where and how much we were educated, who we're married to, where we live, who our friends are, where we were born and when. We might also throw in some of our talents, accomplishments and special skills. But is that who you are? For all of us, the story of who we are began before we had the capacity to form words and memories. Someone told it to us. So, the question we should be asking first is

"Who told you who you are?"

Quite a lot of the facts we believe about ourselves come from the testimony of other people; where we were born, when we were born, how much we weighed and how long we were, whether we were healthy babies or not, what our first word was, when we took our first steps, and so on. Even what we know of our heritage and ancestry comes to us not as indisputable fact but as testimony.

Someone told us the story of us… at least the first chapter.

Who told you who you are?

Without realizing it we grow up with a self identity that is anchored outside our selves, in the stories of others. We describe ourselves by what we have been told of our family history, proclivities, ethnicity and nationality. We identify certain family traits and claim those as though we were genetically predisposed to have them and can't change them. We believe the story we are given. Much of it we learned so early that we didn't think to analyze it. We can't even remember when we began believing what we think is true about us. Even your name was given to you by someone else, and they told you that it was yours.

I was told that I'm of Scottish heritage. On my father's side we're all but 100% Scottish: on my mother's side we have some Yorkshire heritage thrown in. Certain attributes — my skin tone and body build — tend to bear this out, but I could as easily be a Viking or a Russian. Our family is from the South — Georgia and South Carolina — and we were Southern Baptists. I grew up with the impression that my mother's parents were somewhat well-off, not because they were educated, or born into money, or aristocratic, but because they were hard workers. My granddaddy ran a successful sheet metal business in Atlanta.

My mother always spoke of herself as artistic. She wasn't claiming any talent, she just had what she called an 'artistic temperament' and wanted to somehow explain it to herself and others. She told us Kilpatrick kids that we were special and could do anything that we wanted. We believed her. She encouraged me in artistic endeavors. That's likely how I decided to pursue music and drama. What if she had told me a different story about who I was?

My father was orphaned at five years of age. He grew up in the Charleston Orphan House. It's an interesting story but one that isn't necessary here (I tell it in my book *The Art of Being You*) except to touch on the effect his experience had on his outlook, attitudes and what he passed on to his children. His father died, his mother lived but was remote, and he was raised by matrons in the orphan house. Most of the significant adults in his life were aloof, uncaring women. He was accustomed to a strict hierarchical authority structure (perhaps why he chose a career as a chaplain in the Air Force.) I am, to a greater or lesser extent, the product of the nurture of my parents. I can easily see the combination of their influences — of art and ministry — coming together in my life.

So, here I was growing up thinking that I am
- different
- even better, *Special!*
- artistic
- allowed to claim some right to my attitudes and inclinations by a familial predisposition
- unable to change these predispositions about myself

This is a story. More importantly, this is a story that was first told to me by someone else. I joined in as I grew older, certainly, but I didn't make it up and I didn't get it from God. These are not facts. They're not even truths. They are words, and the words became flesh.

I don't remember when I started disliking rainy weather. Maybe it was when I was lost as a kindergarten child in the wet, springtime slushy snow of Mount Holly, New Jersey, where my father was stationed at the time. A mailman picked me up in his mail truck — I was wandering and crying — and drove around until he saw my mother walking in the cold seeming as though she were searching for something or someone. Whether that is the origin of it or not, I never liked rain. I wondered, and would ask out loud, why God made rain. To me it was such a depressing way to water the fields and rivers. Throughout my life, even into adulthood, rainy days always brought me down.

I do remember, though, when and why sunsets started to terrify me. It wasn't really the sunset; it was the time after the sun had gone down when half of the sky is still lit up by the sun and the other is already showing stars. Dusk. It was just a few years after the New Jersey incident and we had moved on to Tachikawa, Japan. My father was late to pick me up from a Boy Scout meeting — my second and last Boy Scout meeting — held at the end of the Air Force Base flight line in the only little building for a half mile. I was too young for the older boys. They treated us smaller ones harshly and the Scout leaders were too busy drinking beer and telling stories to notice. Finally, the meeting was over, all the other parents picked up their sons and the Scout leader locked the door. All the leaders left, too, except one who reluctantly volunteered to stay with me. After awhile he told me he couldn't stay either and he left. I was alone outside that little building, far away from everything, for a long time. I was scared. And the sun went down. All the possibilities that ran through my young mind seemed to center around being abandoned forever. Everything feels like it's going to last forever.

My dad finally came. He apologized, of course, but I didn't look at him for the ride home. I was happy to be safe but still alarmed that something like this could happen to me.

Years later — many years later — when I had been living with these feelings for decades and had come to assume that they were an inalterable part of who I am, I read an article. It said that humans are born with only two innate fears; the fear of loud noises, and the fear of falling. Call it a revelation if you like but I realized then that these two other fears — of rain and of dusk — I had learned. They weren't part of my nature any more than the English language I spoke. I had learned them. And if I had learned them, I knew I could unlearn them. I could change my story, and so I did.

I decided to go out when it rained and thank God for it. I wanted to find the beauty and goodness in it. I reasoned that if my daughter could love rain, so could I. Similarly, In the late afternoon I would pull a chair out to the middle of our deck to watch the sun go down and would stay there through the gloaming. The stars would begin to show themselves and I would rejoice in God's work. I relearned how to experience rain and dusk. I didn't change any facts: they are not mine to change. I changed my story.

The point I am making is that there are so many aspects to our lives that we take for granted as being immutable, unchangeable. The question "who are you?" is easier to answer when our preconceptions about ourselves are accepted as fact rather than story. We become a shorthand version of our true being, living with limitations and definitions that aren't necessarily factual or true or, for that matter, necessary, and almost certainly not liberating.

Yes, there are some fears that are good, such as a fear of God, of the power of nature, of electricity and hot things, but even a good fear exaggerated becomes a bad thing. Fear is a terrible master. Love is better.

Some people abandon the story they've been told of themselves. Maybe they do it for fame, financial gain or power. Maybe it is so limiting, so stained, so soul-crushing that they decide to make up their own story. Actors, musicians and other public figures do this. John Wayne's given name was Marion Anderson. Politician Bill DiBlasio's name was Warren Wilhelm Jr. Charles Manson was born No-Name Manson. They each reinvented themselves. They told another story of who they are. Others make up histories for themselves. One woman I know masqueraded as a Harvard University graduate for decades and was never found out. No one bothered to check. They believed her story.

Leslie Newbiggin, in his book *Proper Confidence*, writes that nearly without exclusion everything we believe is something we heard from someone else. We really don't know that many facts that weren't told us by another person. We trusted that they wouldn't lie to us and we accepted their version of reality. The point he makes is that we believe and trust people, not facts. Facts come to us through people.

Think about it. What do you know about our Solar System that you didn't get from a textbook? What is Pi (and why does it matter)? Who is your father? What is the 'going' price of anything? What is the important news story of the day? Who is God? Really, we know very few facts and a whole lot of stories. This realization can be alarming when you are trying to live a reasoned, rational life. Absolute truth has very little to do with the bank of information we store in our minds. If you think about this it can make you feel as though the very pillars on which you have built your existence are being kicked out from underneath you.

They are.

But the good news is that the universe is not a collection of facts. We have been taught that the universe is guided by a set of principles and these principles, or natural laws, are autonomous. They just are. We accept this as factual. We don't really know *why* they are, we just know *that* they are, like gravity. But what if the story of all creation is more compelling than that? What if what you perceive and believe is incomplete or simply wrong? Is there another way to describe the universe? Let's say that it is one big, wonderful story and there is a Story-teller to believe or disbelieve, and this is all— every molecule and every principle— His story, composed of lots of little stories and truth, not merely facts. And the first step toward finding our place in the universe — that is, in God — is to dismantle and destroy what we think we know — about ourselves and everything else.

CHAPTER 5

"… to root out and to pull down. To destroy and to throw down. To build and to plant." — Jeremiah 1:10

(In this chapter I am writing about our experience within the limitations of our existence in time and space. For instance, when I write that the past is gone I am not speaking of it in the eternal sense. That is a different case, where time and space are circular, or helical, or neither, and all things are always in the continual state of beginning, unfolding, resolving and beginning again. See Rev. 13:8 — "the Lamb slain from the foundation of the world." and John 8:58 — "...before Abraham was, I AM.")

The past is gone. It no longer exists except as a memory, which is to say that it lives on only as a story in the mind. And, since memory is such a fickle thing, the story that lives on in our minds is very often not what we would think of as factual. It is a fiction of our own making. You have probably had the experience of recounting with a friend an occurrence that you both shared and being surprised how different your memories were from each other.

The impact that any occurrence in our past has on us is not being reenacted every moment. It does not live on. Rather, the impact is coming from our own minds. We are causing the effect ourselves. In the course of many years of ministry I have heard stories of abuse and mistreatment that people have endured at the hands of others. If you have been abused or mistreated in the past and that memory is still affecting your life it is because it is being replayed in your own mind. What happened in the past is not still happening. Your former abuser is not still abusing you. You have allowed the memory of that past experience to control and shape your present, but it doesn't exist except in your memory. We act as though the memory of the experience existed apart from us. It does not. We do this to ourselves. We are replaying a story that is no more. Why don't we rewrite our story?

Someone may say that they still carry the scars from some old hurt. Yes, we are all wounded and carry scars, but what story do they tell? The story can be about the loss or about the redemption. Many of us stop the story before we get to the end. God redeems. He makes all things new. Jesus told Thomas to touch His scars after the resurrection. He still carried the wounds but the story they told was one of power, of overcoming, of resurrection, not just of pain and death. In God's telling every story has a good and noble end. *He will reconcile all things to Himself*, Paul tells us in Colossians 1:19. All things will 'make sense' and come to a joyful, triumphant conclusion in His good story. As a friend of mine told me, "if it's funny later, it's funny now." And we can say *if it's good later, it's good now.*

The future is our projection of probabilities. Nothing we might think about the future is sure to happen. When we envision what may come we are predicting it. It doesn't exist any more than the past does. I once ran through a glass door, shattering it and cutting my arms up pretty badly. It so confused me that I didn't know how to respond for several minutes. What I had projected — that I would push the door open, get in the car with my family and go have a nice picnic — didn't happen. I spent the rest of the day in the emergency room getting stitched up. My projection of the future never happened. The future does not exist.

All there is is this present moment. We live on the knife edge of the experience of reality and it never slips away, or slips away at lightning speed. So very quickly the present becomes a memory and ceases to be, giving way to another present. All you have is this moment. If you are going to do something, this is your moment. All the plans we have for the future are merely projections, but so many things can come along to change them. We make our plans for the future and forget to take advantage of the present. If you are going to be in His presence, do it now. If you plan to pray, do it now. God the eternal comes to us only in the present, not in the past or the future. This is a significant part of the meaning of the name of God — *I Am*.

Jesus delayed coming to Bethany to visit the family of His friend Lazarus. He knew and had told the disciples that Lazarus was dead. When He got close to the town, Martha came out to meet Him and said to Him *"Lord, if you had been here, my brother would not have died."* (John 11:20-27) She immediately pushed the conversation into the past. Jesus replied to her that her brother would rise again. In her response to this Martha jumped into the future: *"I know that he will rise again in the resurrection at the last day."* She skipped right over the present moment. Jesus brings her forcefully into the present by saying *"I am the resurrection and the life... Do you believe Me?"* Martha seems willing to blame her brother's death on Jesus' delay in arriving. She also seems to have a general belief in the resurrection of the dead on the day of judgement, but she doesn't seem to grasp that God is the *I AM* of the present moment and that He does what He does in the present. He raised Lazarus from the dead that day.

You may ask why God didn't help you in your past troubles — *"where were you, God?!"* You may be waiting to be set free on that last day when He will wipe away all our tears and we will be forever changed. But is it possible that you could invite Him into your present moment and see Him transform your life now? The *now* is where the *I AM* lives and moves. The kingdom of heaven is here, now. God the *I AM* is here, now.

So why does God give us the perception of past and future? Why do we move through space and time like this? It is for the formation of our character. An imagination becomes an intention, an intention becomes an act, an act becomes a habit and a habit becomes character. The disciplines of the church as acts are given to us to shape our actions in the present moment and those actions become our character. When they become an end in themselves and cease to be the means for us to live and celebrate His presence in this moment they become, like manna, unhealthy. We will cover this in a later chapter but anything that begins by representing something else and then becomes a Thing of its own takes the place of God Himself and is dangerous. The practice of the disciplines of the church can never take the place of God. They must always lead us to Him only, in the present moment.

You can only be one place at a time. If you are here, you are not there. For you, there is no other place but here. This is also true of God. He is here. In truth, He is more here than you are. He is holding the very particles of creation together. He is present in everything in every way, at the most inward and outward point, in the most primal, basic sense.

God is here and there is no there.

He does not move through space like we do. He *is* the space. When we vacate one spot and assume another we have exchanged there for here, and the former here becomes there. But God never leaves one spot to take up another. The theological word for it is

Omnipresent. He is here and there is no there. He never moves. He never vacates His position. We talk about God moving — and it is a useful metaphor — but it can limit our understanding of His true being. It can make us think that He is *in* the universe when the truth is that He *is* the universe, or the universe is in Him. All His creation is in Him. Romans 11:36 says *"For of Him and through Him and to Him are all things..."* God never changes. He is the same yesterday, today and forever. There is no shadow of turning in Him. He holds all things together. In Him all things consist. He is all in all. One of the curious and joyful truths is that the never-changing God presents Himself to us in an ever-changing universe.

He is all in all.

Can you see why David seemed to lament that he couldn't get away from God? *"Where can I go from Your Spirit? Or where can I flee from Your presence? If I ascend into heaven, You are there; If I make my bed in hell, You are there."* (Ps. 139:7-8) There is no place that is not full of His presence. To know His presence is not a matter of movement, it is a matter of perception. You are now in His presence whether you perceive Him or not. Or you might say that *He* is always in *your* presence, with you every moment everywhere, seen or unseen.

Jesus met a woman at Jacob's Well. (John 4:5-38) He told her things about her life that made her think He was a prophet. Then she asked Him a question about the proper place to worship God: *"Our fathers worshipped on this mountain, and you Jews say that in Jerusalem is the place where one ought to worship."* Both places were not where she was at the moment. She was asking "*there* or *there?*" The whole of Jesus' response to her is very interesting, but I want to pick out one part that Christians quote a lot. Jesus ties time and place together into the *here and now* when He says to her *"But the hour is coming, and now is, when the true worshipers will worship the Father in spirit and truth..."* Neither spirit nor truth is determined by place or time. We make appointments with God to, say, meet Him for devotions tomorrow morning in our living room, but He calls us out of the future and out of the past, out of *there* and *there,* to this moment and this place. Give Him this moment in this place. Now and here. It's all you have.

In 2 Kings 6, when Elisha and his assistant were surrounded by an enemy army that came to kill him, Elisha told his man that there were more with them than there were against them. I can imagine the dismay in his assistant. He couldn't understand how the two of them were more than the army outside. But then Elisha prayed a significant prayer — *"Open his eyes."* Change his perception. The Lord answered Elisha's prayer and the eyes of his assistant now saw the flaming armies of God surrounding the enemy. *Nothing changed about the situation except his ability to perceive.* Many times we pray for a change of situation when what we really need is a change of perception. There is often so much going on in the invisible realm that would change our attitude greatly and God wants to increase our ability to perceive it and, even when we don't, to trust Him. Paul tells us in 2 Corinthians 4:18 *"...we do not look at the things which are seen, but at the things which are not seen..."*

John 12:2-29 shows us Jesus on His way to the cross. He is walking along with His disciples and other followers and words are dropping like gold from His lips. At the end of one comment He prays a four word prayer — *"Father, glorify Your name."* A voice comes from heaven saying *"I have both glorified it and will glorify it again."*

John understood Who spoke and what was said and recorded it for us. He also recorded that there were some who thought an angel had spoken to Him while others thought it had thundered. In this story we have three levels of perception in the same situation. Some people know His voice and understand Him. Some people are aware that there is something spiritual going on but aren't quite sure what it is — an angel, perhaps. Then there are those that seem to have no spiritual awareness or understanding at all. They hear thunder.

When God speaks to you there will always be those who will try to convince you that it's only thunder. They aren't doing this because they are necessarily evil; it's all they hear.

Which group do you want to be in? It is possible to train your spiritual perception, just as it happened that your physical perceptions were trained by reason of use. Babies learn to hear and see and to recognize and interpret the shapes and sounds they perceive. When the Bible calls us sincere babes the inference is that the same growth process babies experience in the visible physical realm is available to us in the invisible spiritual realm. The more you use any gift of God, the more you understand how to use it. I love 2 Corinthians 3:18 that talks about us having unveiled faces. The more we desire and seek Him the more He unveils our spiritual senses. The prayer we sing that asks God to *'open the eyes of my heart'* also takes on a greater significance to us. It is God's desire that we should live in the invisible realm as we do the visible — the heavenly realm as the physical. Remember the line in the Lord's Prayer that says *'on earth as it is in heaven.'* This is not fanciful religious talk on God's part. *"Your kingdom…on earth." Your will…on earth."* These are expressions of God's will for us. More importantly, in the context of His teaching on how we ought to pray, they are Him telling us that we should actively seek and ask for these. The deep desire and the petition for God's good gifts will always be fulfilled. There is something to the Beatitude that says *'blessed are those who hunger and thirst…'* God says there is a blessing in the hunger and the thirst — the deep desire. The lack of, and the earnest desire for, something of God is the beginning of receiving it. And what God gives is not outside Him. He always gives of Himself, from within Himself.

He gives Himself.

CHAPTER 6

"If a person wishes to be sure of the road they tread upon, they must close their eyes and walk in the dark." — St. John of the Cross

A few years ago, after having gone to bed, my wife and I were lying on our backs in the dark chatting. I had my eyes closed. Sometime into our conversation I opened my eyes and saw that the room was filled with a cloud — of smoke, I assumed, because we have fireplaces, and my first thought was that one of them was not drawing quite well. I told Cindy about it and was preparing to go take care of the problem. Before I could, though, Cindy grabbed my arm and asked *"What do you see?"* I told her again that the room was filled with smoke and that I was looking at it. She held me even tighter and said *"I don't see anything."* I was incredulous. I reached my hand up and swirled the smoke around and said *"Don't you see that?!"* She said no. She saw no smoke.

I moved my eyes around to make sure it wasn't something cloudy in my eyes. It wasn't. I reached up again and waved my hand, disturbing the cloud. It was there and I could interact with it, but only I could see it. I wasn't in deep prayer or feeling anything mystical at the time. There was no overt sense of the presence of God. Nothing. Just a cloud above me. This happened every night for a long time. Even when I was in a hotel room somewhere else I would see the cloud. I saw it during daylight hours as well. Again, it didn't come with any special sensation and to this day I have no explanation for why it happened or what its purpose was. I do know, though, that it created a desire in me to study clouds in the Bible. I found that there are many more references to clouds in the Bible than I remembered and they pop up in some unexpected places. I believe they are significant. They tell us something about the nature of God and how He relates to us.

Sometimes as we read the Bible we skip over phrases that don't seem too important to us. Regarding clouds, maybe we've been influenced by those Renaissance paintings that depict Jesus in the clouds surrounded by winged, flying babies. Everything in the painting seems to be more fanciful than real. So when we read about clouds in the Bible we might subconsciously put them in the same fanciful category as those cute little cherubs. But there is not any wasted word in the Bible. There is no extraneous material there. Every word and image has meaning and is part of the symmetry of truth and revelation contained in all of it. Here is a partial list of cloud references in the Bible.

Gen. 9:13-17 — *"I set my rainbow in the cloud...the rainbow shall be in the cloud... This is the sign of the covenant"*
Ex. 13:21-22 — *"And the Lord went before them by day in a pillar of cloud..."*
Ex. 16:10 — *"...the glory of the Lord appeared in the cloud."*
Ex. 19:9 — *"...I come to you in the thick cloud..."*
Ex. 19:16 — *"...thunderings and lightnings, and a thick cloud on the mountain..."*

Ex. 19:18 — *"...Mount Sinai was completely in smoke, because the Lord descended upon it in fire."*

Ex. 24:16 — *"...He called to Moses out of the midst of the cloud."*

Ex. 34:5 — *"Now the Lord descended in the cloud..."*

Ex. 40:34 — *"Then the cloud covered the tabernacle of meeting, and the glory of the Lord filled the tabernacle."*

Lev. 16:2 — *"...for I will appear in the cloud above the mercy seat."*

Num. 9:15 — *"Now on the day that the tabernacle was raised up, the cloud covered the tabernacle, the tent of the Testimony."*

Num. 11:25 — *"Then the Lord came down in the cloud, and spoke to him..."*

1 Kings 8:12 — *"Then Solomon spoke: The Lord said He would dwell in the dark cloud."*

Ps. 97:2 — *"Clouds and darkness surround Him..."*

Ps; 99:7 — *"He spoke to them in the cloudy pillar..."*

Eze. 1:4 — *"...a great cloud with raging fire engulfing itself..."*

Eze. 10:3-4 — *"...and the cloud filled the inner court...Then the glory of the Lord went up from the cherub...and the house was filled with the cloud..."*

Matt. 17:5 — *"...a bright cloud overshadowed them; and suddenly a voice came out of the cloud, saying, "This is My Beloved Son, in whom I am well pleased. Hear Him!"*

(Also see Mark 9:7 & Luke 9:34-35)

Mt. 24:30 — *"...they will see the Son of Man coming on the clouds of heaven with power and great glory."*

Acts 1:9-11 — *"...He was taken up, and a cloud received Him out of their sight...This same Jesus...will so come in like manner as you saw Him go up into heaven."*

Rev. 1:7 — *"Behold, He is coming with clouds, and every eye will see Him..."*

Rev. 11:11 — *"...and they ascended to heaven in a cloud, and their enemies saw them."*

Rev. 14:14 — *"...and behold, a white cloud, and on the cloud sat one like the Son of Man..."*

There seem to be many references to God being in, coming in and speaking from the cloud. In the New Testament, the word translated cloud in all but one verse is actually the word 'cloudiness.' Only in Hebrews 12:1 when talking about the 'cloud of witnesses' is the actual root word — cloud — used. God seems to prefer to present Himself to us in cloudiness. Why would that be? Is there any clue to His character and purposes in this? I believe there is.

A few years ago one of my sons called to say he was asking God for some clarity on a decision he was to make. In a burst of candor I said "All the best with that clarity thing!" He asked me what I meant and I told him that I had never had clarity on any major decision I had ever made. I was envious of those people who testified that *"the Lord spoke to me."* I felt like a second class Christian for not having ever had the Lord "speak" to me on any of the decisions I faced in my life.

in 1971 when I told my fellow Jesus People friends that I was engaged to Cindy at the age of eighteen (married at nineteen) they were very concerned. We were a deeply committed, spiritually idealistic bunch and were taught to expect Jesus to speak to us and guide us in every decision we made, even to the choice of which socks to wear that day! I was a dismal failure at this but wanted it to happen to me like they said it happened to them. I was also a bit of a contrarian. So when they asked me in their quivering, overly spiritual way *"Brother, are you sure this is the will of God?"* I replied *"Nope. But if I could wake up next to her every day for the rest of my life I would be a happy man."* Oh, this didn't help things at all. They wanted clarity and all I had was cloudiness. They wanted divine guidance and all I had was a strong, godly desire and my own firm intentions. I'm still married to Cindy. Sadly, some of the marriages that were formed because 'God spoke' to them to do it ended in divorce.

Let's go back to Moses on Mount Sinai. At one point, in Exodus 33, Moses wants to see the face of God. Early in the chapter He tells Moses that His Presence will go with them. When Moses presses Him the Lord says *"You cannot see My face; for no man shall see me, and live."* (v. 20) Instead, Moses and the people of Israel were to follow the cloud. Moses wanted clarity and God gave him cloudiness. We want to see His face. We even ask Him to show us His face. We want things to be clear and they're not. All we see is fog, mist, clouds.

Note that though God would not show His face He nonetheless assured Moses that His Presence would go with them. Jesus seems to reaffirm this in John 14 when He says that He will never leave us or forsake us. God keeps calling us to be *with* Him. It's about Presence. Sadly, much of the preaching I hear today is not about Presence but about Imitation. We're trying oh, so hard to be like Jesus. We're given methods and principles and habits that we are told will help us to be His hands and His feet. We talked about this in an earlier chapter, but the call of God through the ages is to be *with* Him, not *like* Him.

Perhaps we're afraid to be with Him because we think we're not enough like Him.

Chapter 7

There is a second dangerous presumption in the question "What would Jesus do?" It is that we presume we are called to try and reason what we think His response in a given circumstance might be (were He actually here) and then to *do what He would do*. This would certainly be a good approach if all you had was the Bible. It would be a good approach if you assumed that 1) He wasn't here and 2) you were called to "be" Jesus to the people you meet. But this adds a layer of pretension to our lives, which is the beginning of hypocrisy. When we do this, we're not living *with* Him, we're just trying to *act like* Him. Our character can take a back seat to our actions in this scenario. I don't think it's any wonder that some Christian leaders have been exposed as having dark and decaying inner lives while having 'successful' public ministries. We only expected them to act like they thought Jesus would act. The underlying Cessationist theology in this is evident and alarming. I will make a couple of observations:

Jesus is here.

You are not Jesus.

Do you have any argument with those observations? Perhaps we should also state that the Living God is willing and able to be engaged and to do miraculous things in this present moment. Now, *that* may separate us into two groups. On the one side we'll have the ones who believe that God has gone inactive and silent. If we ask Him anything He'll just point (if we believe He still points) at the Bible. Like the idols of the Old Testament, He is mute and unmoving. On the other side we'll have those that are mystics, who believe that God is alive, present, fully engaged and willing to communicate, albeit in His cloudy way. Of course, I recognize that there are dangers and excesses possible in both approaches. While it seems the mystical dangers get more coverage I believe that the excesses of Cessationism are equally, even more, dangerous. I don't mind throwing out the bath water but I certainly want to keep the baby and, for myself, I'd prefer a little danger with my abundant life over a guarantee of security in exchange for some placid, low level existence in service to an insipid religious system. Besides, this is not what you were created for or called to experience. Jesus did not call you to join a new religion, He called you to be *fully alive!*

Jesus condemned the religion of the Pharisees and Sadducees not so much because they were wrong but because they weren't *alive*. He called them sepulchers with dead men's bones. He compared the static life of religious observances with the dynamic life that was *"pressed down, shaken together and running over."* The reason He lashed out so vociferously against their approach was because their standing with God hinged on their efforts. If they kept all the statutes as they interpreted them then they could take some pride in their own work. Through the ages people have wanted to accomplish their religious duties with some sort of method, regimen or practice. We seem to prefer principles and practices over Presence. Or, to put it the way the

Apostle Paul did, we incline toward the Letter rather than the Spirit.

In 2 Corinthians chapter 3, Paul contrasts the Letter and the Spirit by beginning in verse three with this: *"clearly you are an epistle of Christ… written <u>not with ink</u> but by the Spirit of the Living God…"* Because of the way we have been taught, we push this section of the Bible off as a condemnation of the Jewish Law, but what Paul is saying is broader than that. It is the same theme that he explores in Galatians — *"having begun in the Spirit, are you now being made perfect by the flesh?"* (Gal. 3:3) When he says in 2 Cor. 3:6 that the letter kills but the Spirit gives life he is saying that ANY written system of religious principles that you think will increase your standing with and approval from God will kill you. You create this kind of system if you take away from your religious beliefs an active relationship with the Living God — the Ghost of God — and meet Him only as a character in a book, even if He is the most excellent character in the most wonderful book.

Paul says in 1 Cor. 1:18 that the message of the cross is foolishness to those who are perishing and power to those who are being saved. In the previous verse he is concerned with the cross being made of no effect by what? — by mere wisdom of words. He goes on to say that the point is that no flesh (human) should glory or boast in His presence. In Galatians 5:11 Paul says that the cross is offensive. Don't for a moment think that he means that only for the religious Jews. The cross of Jesus is offensive to *every* religion and to *every* religious person because it liberates people from religious observances and calls them to stop living by the *Letter* and to live in the *Spirit*. The *Letter* can be, and ought to be, understood as describing any practice of religion, Christianity included, that is based primarily on a written code.

In large part 'Christianity' has become just one more of the religious expressions of humankind. (I am often saddened that it was labeled, organized and institutionalized like it has been. However, even in this diminished form 'Christianity' is superior to all other religions. The same is true of it as is said about democracy — it is the worst form of government, except for all the rest.) Christianity as a religious system has taken its place next to Judaism, Islam, Hinduism and Buddhism as one of the "great religions of the world." *How did this happen?!* How did the most exciting, momentous thing to ever happen in the history of the world become so weak and uninteresting?

As Dorothy L. Sayers observed, *"The people who hanged Christ never, to do them justice, accused Him of being a bore — on the contrary; they thought Him too dynamic to be safe. It has been left for later generations to muffle up that shattering personality and surround Him with an atmosphere of tedium."*

One of the ways that the weakening and emasculation of Christianity happened is that we got ourselves a book. Christianity became a book-based religious system of practices. It's not the book that has done harm but what we have made of it and done with it. All religions start as movements with a mystic leader and at some time in their history collate the teachings and codes into written form. The Yazidis are doing that right now — collecting the oral tales from their religious traditions into a holy book. *Do you see the danger here?!*

"This is not a pipe!"

Again let me say that I am not at all questioning the veracity, authenticity or infallibility of the Bible. I am saying that the greatest danger we face is right under our noses, which is to love the book more than the God of the book.

Just as we will see presently in the story of the serpent that Hezekiah destroyed, the Holy Book that was meant to serve us, to help us live in His presence, show us His character and provide a touchstone for revelation has become the Thing Itself. Tragically, there are pastors who love the Bible more than they love Jesus. They prefer the Letter to the Spirit. My father called it bibliolatry. This is, in my opinion, the most subtle and greatest danger to the people of the Way. We choose to only see Jesus in the book and not to see Him — His Ghost — alive in this moment. If ever there was a recipe for inauthentic, insipid powerlessness, this is it.

Let"s jump four hundred years from Moses to the young king Hezekiah. In 2 Kings 18 we are told that he did three things when he began his reign. He removed the pagan worship sites and cut down their pillars, removed the image of Asherah (a pagan goddess), and broke into pieces the bronze serpent that Moses had made. It's easy to understand why this godly young man did the first two things: he wanted to rid the land of the worship of false gods. But why would he destroy a four hundred year old relic and remembrance from the days of Moses and the miraculous journey from Egypt to the promised land?

He destroyed it because the serpent had ceased to be a representation of God's good work in their past and had become a thing in itself. It had become an idol — Nehushtan — and the Jewish people offered incense to it. Can you see the similarity to the Magritte painting? The representation had become the Thing. It was no longer connected or pointing to the Living God. While they could not see God, they could see the serpent. It gave them clarity. It was an object they could see and over time it moved from representing and remembering God to being a god itself. This is the inherent danger in making a depiction of God or an object of devotion. We develop a love and fear for the image, object or book more than the God it represents and serves.

Let's jump ahead once more, to the Mount of Transfiguration. (Matt. 17, Mark 9, Luke 9) Jesus is transfigured before Peter, James and John. (The idea of transfiguration is an interesting study of its own.) Moses and Elijah appear to them, talking with Jesus. And there is that cloud again, enveloping the whole scene. Peter makes a suggestion that they should make three tabernacles — that is, religious objects — to commemorate and memorialize the event. Just as at Mount Sinai, a voice comes from the cloud, and it tells them that *"this is My Beloved Son, in whom I am well pleased. Hear Him!"* To my mind, God is forcefully steering Peter away from the objectification and directing his attention to the person of God in the cloud. Can you imagine if they had built those three tabernacles what we might have made of them over the centuries? I would venture to say that there might be a grand cathedral built on the site with a long line of people each day waiting — and paying — to touch the tabernacles and receive a blessing. We might even have an offshoot of Christianity dedicated to the veneration of the objects themselves — the Church of the Three Tabernacles. We might fashion "Three Tabernacles" jewelry out of silver or gold and hang it on a necklace. Worse has happened.

We want clarity. We want to understand what God is doing in our lives. We want Him to shine a light on our paths. We want life to make sense but God is not helping us to get it. GK Chesterton said *"The trouble with life is that it almost makes sense."* God doesn't seem to care to help us make sense of things. What He calls us to is not clarity but trust. A friend sent me a poem that said something about us wanting God to shine a light on our path while God is wanting us to put our hands in His and walk with Him into the darkness. If you think you're living in a cloud, wandering in a fog, you are not alone. That is where God lives.

Chapter 8

Most of our prayer times seem to be spent asking God for two things — information and provision. We want information — to know what His will is for our lives. We put our needs and the needs of others before Him and ask Him for provision — money, strength, comfort, healing. Neither of these kinds of prayers are bad but there is something better. You were called a child of God, not an employee; a friend and a lover, not a servant. You are not a line worker in God's factory. If your prayer time is spent merely reciting a requisitions list of what you need, or need to know, to fulfill your job, you are missing the central thing for which you were created; fellowship and intimacy with God. Again, the Westminster Confession says that the *"chief end of man is to glorify God and enjoy Him forever."* In modern times many churches have replaced this with *"to know Him and to make Him known."* In the first case the focus is *to* God alone, and in the second it is split — *to* God and *for* God — so that there is the introduction of a humanistic element. In doing this we have written ourselves into God's responsibility! We are going to do something *for* God. We have created a job for ourselves — the Great Commission. Through the ages man seems to have a preference for doing something *for* God rather than being *with* Him, but Mary chose the better part, not Martha. We have made the chief end of man to evangelize the world, but we've got the wrong end of the stick. Evangelism is not a goal, it's a result. It is what naturally, or supernaturally, happens when the Church lives in the presence of the Living God and practices the character and power of God among themselves in community and in view of the world around them. The "chief end of man" is not a responsibility or a job, no matter how noble or necessary it may seem, it's a relationship; *"to glorify God and enjoy Him forever."*

This misunderstanding is due in no small part to our reinterpretation of the word 'witness.' We have made 'witnessing' into a special kind of religious activity. We go out to 'share our faith.' We are told that if we don't tell people about Jesus and have them 'pray the sinner's prayer' then their blood will be on our heads. Our idea of witnessing in these modern times looks more like a forced propaganda or sales campaign than anything. But what is the true meaning of the word? A witness is someone who saw and/or heard something and can vouch for its genuineness. Whatever happened, a witness had to be there for it. John says it this way in 1 John 1, *"That ...which we have heard, which we have seen with our own eyes, which we have looked upon, and our hands have handled, concerning the Word of life...we declare to you."* This is first hand experience, not hearsay. It's not even a quote from a good sermon. John is saying *"I was there for it and that's what I'm telling you about!"*

If you were called to be a witness in court the judge would ask for your testimony. If you began by saying "I believe —" he would interrupt you, have that stricken from the record and instruct you that what he wanted to hear was not what you believe but what you experienced. Period. If he asked you to identify someone and you said "I believe —" he would again tell you that he's not interested in what you believe: he is only interested in your first hand knowledge and experience of the person in question. Sadly, for many Christians, witnessing is a second hand story. They're telling what they believe, not what they know for themselves. They heard it from someone or they read about it in the Bible and they repeated it. It might as well be a sales pitch. *"Would you like to buy the car today?" "Would you like to ask Jesus into your heart today?"* I don't remember reading anywhere in the Bible where the Christians asked anyone that question. There is no mention of anyone praying the sinner's prayer or accepting Jesus as a personal Lord and Savior. I do, however, remember reading that people were stirred so strongly that they asked *"what must I do to be saved?"* I do remember reading in John 9 about that blind man who told the religious leaders that he didn't know too much about Jesus, but he did know that he was once blind but now could see. Again, evangelism is not a goal but a result. What a great Church it would be if the Alongsiders glorified and enjoyed God and the onlookers couldn't help but ask how they could have it, too!

I understand that in Mark 16:15-18 Jesus said that we should go into all the world. We think we know these verses well enough, but it's still worth going over the whole passage. He tells us to preach to every creature. (Literalists, explain that word *creature*, please.) Then He tells us that those who believe and are baptized will be saved. There seems to be something missing. Jesus skips right over that middle moment between preaching and baptizing. There is no altar call, no sinner's prayer, no asking into the heart. Our responsibilities precede and follow the moment of belief that ought to happen in their lives, but we don't seem to be called to 'close the sale.' We preach. If they believe, we baptize them. What happens in between in their spirits is in the hands of God. You may think that I'm being picky but I think it's important to know that that part of it is *God's* work, not ours, lest anyone should boast.

Let's go on, because that is not the end of what has come to be known as the Great Commission. Most Christians stop with the "preach and baptize" part, as though that were sufficient to support our *'to know Him and to make Him known'* theology. But Jesus goes on to say that there are signs that will follow those who believe and He enumerates some of them: *"In My name they will cast out demons; they will speak with new tongues; and they will take up serpents; and if they drink anything deadly, it will by no means hurt them; they will lay hands on the sick, and they will recover."* Tell me, how can we accept one part of this saying without accepting all of it? It's either all great or none great. And if the second part, where the miracles are, was only for the Apostles, how can we say that the first part is somehow still in force for all believers? It seems clear to me that we are empowered to preach, baptize, cast out demons, speak in tongues, be unaffected by poisons and heal the sick. We are called to live with His power and, as a result, people will believe. In other words, *be* a true witness, don't *do* witnessing. What will give power to what you say is not a lurid testimony but the ring of truth. Tell what you have experienced of Jesus and leave it at that, even if it's plain and simple, because the truth is better than anything you could make up. Just remember that blind man in John 9.

Jesus, in John 17:3, gives us a clear definition of eternal life and it is not a job, a length of days, or something we'll experience later in the 'sweet by and by.' It is a quality of relationship. *"This is eternal life, that they might know You, the only true God, and Jesus Christ whom You have sent."* The word 'know' here is the same word used in Matthew chapter one when it tells us that Joseph did not 'know' Mary but took her as his wife. It's *that* intimate. It's the same word that Jesus uses in Matthew chapter seven when He says *"depart from Me; I never knew you."* It's *that* important. He's describing something beyond acquaintance; a friendship so close as to be familiar with the habits, gestures and expressions, even thoughts, of the other.

I hear people complain sometimes — "you've got to know someone to get in there." They will describe how a person made it to the top in their career because they knew somebody. They seem to resent the fact that the successful ones 'know someone.' Instead, they want everyone to be judged merely by their good performance in their job. What they are missing is this —

This is how the universe works!

Everything is accomplished through relationships. And what they complain about is true at the heart of all creation, in the very center of authority, in heaven: *you've got to know someone to get in there.* There is no entrance exam. There is no measure of performance or ability. You didn't have to sign up and get your name on a list. It begins and it ends with who you know.

Someone may say, ah, but we will be judged by our fruit. That is true, but tell me how fruitfulness is an exertion or a work. Plants don't take up the job or responsibility of bearing fruit. It's what naturally happens when they are well planted and well nurtured. Jesus, in comparing us to branches of the vine, tells us simply to stay connected to Him. Remain in Him and you will be well planted, well nurtured and will *naturally* produce fruit. Remaining or abiding in Him reminds me of that word *mone* — staying — we talked about earlier.

Now, back to John 14 and Jesus preparing His *Alongsiders* for life after the Ascension. For three years they have had a God they can see in the person of Jesus. They have walked with Him, talked with Him and eaten with Him. But He tells them that this season is coming to an end. He keeps repeating to them that He is not leaving them but that He will take another form — a Ghost — and they should be prepared for this change. In a poignant verse 18, He says *"I will not leave you orphans: I will come to you."* He keeps emphasizing that, though He will be with them, His form will be different than it had been. Verse 19 — *"A little while longer and the world will see Me no more, but you will see Me."* In verse 21 He says that to the one who loves Him *"I will manifest Myself to him."*

This does not sound like a person who is saying *"sometime in the future some of you will write your memoirs and I will then communicate only through those and some other treatises by some other men."* He doesn't say here that the Holy Bible will lead us into all truth. He puts that on His Ghost. Again, I am not demeaning the Bible or taking anything away from its inerrancy. I believe it all. That's precisely why I believe what Jesus is saying here in John. As someone has wryly said, the Trinity is not the Father, Son and Holy Bible, but that seems to be the practical theology much of the Western church embraces. Frankly, we seem to be afraid of the Ghost of God. We have, for the most part, written the Ghost out of our experience. We look to the Letter for guidance rather than the Spirit. It bears repeating that Jesus told us in John 16:13 *"when He, the Spirit of truth has come, He will guide you into all truth…"*

All this talk of ghosts and clouds is anathema to the rational, reasonable, logical Christianity we inherited from the Enlightenment. We have learned to expect that everything about our faith, from discipleship to fruitfulness, can be passed on and learned through teaching and knowledge. But so often something happens in our lives — something unexpected and unexplainable — that upsets our tidy theology and we find that not everything is rational, logical or even reasonable. We are forced to face and embrace a mystery. This is the gift of God to us. He is calling us to Himself…

…in the cloud…

…the cloud of His presence.

Chapter 9

Glory be to the Father
And to the Son
And to the Holy Ghost
God in three Persons,
Blessed Trinity

I read an interview recently with a leading American pastor in which he referred to the Holy Spirit as the "friend of Jesus." I hear some Christians refer to the Ghost of God simply as "Holy Spirit," as though it was a name (first name *Holy*, last name *Spirit*) and not a description. In the pastor's case this is wildly bad theology, but both approaches give a wrong understanding of God.

I had a conversation with a Jewish man about his view of Christianity and his first observation was that we were different from the Jews because we believed in three gods. I did my best to disabuse him of this notion but it was to no avail. He simply couldn't accept the idea of three God-persons who were still, somehow, one God. I'm not sure even Christians can reconcile this seeming contradiction in their minds, either, and I'm fairly sure most of them don't care enough to try. In our emphasis on the Three Persons, we seem somehow to have lost the essential unity of God expressed in Deuteronomy 6:4 —

"Hear, O Israel: The Lord our God, the Lord is one!"

In my opinion we have become a bit too trinitarian, or at the least our understanding of the trinity is so vague as to be meaningless or misleading. I know that there have been various heresies and theological streams through the centuries that claimed that the three persons of the trinity were manifestations, emanations, offices, administrations or aspects of God, and I'm not interested here in going through them and refuting, supporting or even discussing them. I am saying that, for the most part, the misunderstanding of the Trinity comes from a mishandling of the images in the Bible. When we expect a metaphor to be the thing it represents — that is, when we make a literal interpretation of something in the

Bible that was meant to be figurative — we straight off set our understanding in the wrong direction, and get War Drobe, or Spare Oom. The truth is, though, that no matter what we believe about the Trinity, God is still One — unified, single and unchanging.

We have become so comfortable with the individuality of the Father and the Son and the Holy Spirit that we, like the pastor, think of them as separate beings. They're just eternal pals in our vague theology, and we're not really sure why the Father and the Son asked that other One — the Ghost — to join them. Perhaps we can clear some of this up by remembering again that words are metaphors. They are not the things they represent. As an example, God the Father is not a father in the same sense that we think of an earthly one. He isn't married, doesn't go to work or hang out in the garage or watch sports on Sunday afternoons. The concept of a *Father* is given to us as a way of understanding Him because we need something we already know about to relate Him to. We know what fathers ought to be and do and we see in God the Father the perfect embodiment of all the noble and good attributes of perfect fatherhood.

Similarly, God as the Son and as the Ghost are also metaphors. These are given to us so that we can understand God through things we already know. This same approach can also be seen in the way Jesus spoke about the kingdom of God. He told us the *"kingdom of God is like…"* He used pictures and relationships we had at hand to show us something about God and His kingdom. Jesus is not really a vine and we're not branches. The kingdom of God is not really a mustard seed. These are the individual strokes of a paint brush that, when seen together, form an image and show us something of God. There is no way to talk about anything without comparing or likening it to things we already know about.

How would you explain the mist of fog to someone who has never seen it? You might say it's like a cloud come down around us, or that it's like the smoke from a fire that doesn't rise but hangs in the air. You might say that it can make it difficult to see clearly and you can feel it on your skin. None of these alone are sufficient to describe the mist but, taken together, they might come close enough. If you told the someone that the mist is actually the same thing as ice or water you'd likely confuse the matter in their minds. It might seem easier, at least at first, and we might be tempted to deal with mist as though it had no relation to the flowing stream or the frozen pond, and yet mist is not *like* water, it *is* water, and water is not *like* ice, it *is* ice. All three are one. Each one is the others in a different form.

The Jews missed knowing that Jesus was the Messiah not because they were oblivious or blind or didn't care. Jews have always been, and even are to this day, on eager watch for the Messiah. They were indeed looking for Him, just in the wrong places. They had a different expectation of the form He would take and had come to believe so strongly in their interpretation of that form that they couldn't see it any other way. Is it possible that the same has happened to us? Our expectations of what form God will take can make it hard for us to see Him when He is at work in our lives. As I frequently told the folks I pastored, I don't want to change *what* you see in the Bible, I want to change *how* you see it. I want to change your glasses. I want you to understand and see what is there in a new — and ancient — way.

As Dr. Michael Heiser points out in his book *The Unseen Realm*, we read the Bible through a modern lens and through our own cultural understanding; many times not at all in the same way that it was written. Our interpretations are often clouded by the change in meaning words go through over time or in translation. Some of these changes are due to the general change in language from generation to generation and some are because the meanings were theologically interpreted to have a definition that was not originally intended. The word *mansion* we have mentioned before serves as a good example of this. The good Christian understanding of *faith* might be another. Faith variously means a body of theological belief, a general hope, a strong belief or an unshakable certainty. It is the last one that is the meaning used by Paul and the other New Testament writers. Paul never referred to faith as meaning the body of Christian theology as oppose to the *Jewish faith* or the *Muslim faith*. As Hebrews says, faith *is* substance, not a hope for substance: it *is* evidence, not a believing for evidence. How we understand this one word significantly affects our experience and expectations of God.

As I have mentioned, these metaphors of Father, Son and Ghost are given to us so that we might know God through something we already have at hand. God the Father: got it. God the Son: like fathers, we know about sons and can easily make the connection. But when we get to God the Ghost we find ourselves in strange territory. We don't know that much about ghosts and aren't very comfortable thinking about them. And, from the way we have been taught to read the Bible, we think that we're courting danger by even considering the possibility. Besides, aren't we logical, rational beings? Do we actually believe in ghosts? In most churches the Ghost of God is, at the least, just a warm feeling in your heart and, at the most, more like the Force in Star Wars. For many the Ghost is an emotion, a passion, a stirring, but not a person, and not the actual Person of God. Isn't he just the eternal friend of Jesus?

Throughout much of this book when referring to the Holy Spirit I have intentionally used the phrase *Ghost of God.* There are several reasons for this. First, I want to remind us of His ghostliness. There are ghosts — that is, spirit-beings without bodies — and He is one. Second, I want to shake up our thinking to make sure that we really are considering it and have got the right idea about this. Third, I want to emphasize that the Holy Spirit is not the friend of God but God Himself. He is the Ghost of God.

Ice, water, mist.

When Jesus is preparing the *Alongsiders* in John 14 for their life after the Ascension, He speaks about the Ghost of God like we might about the mist. He tells them in verse sixteen that He will ask the Father and the Father will send the One called Alongside to abide with them forever. We might say that the mist — or, shall we say, the cloud? — will appear around them and will envelope them. We might say that in a little while they won't see the stream but they will see the cloud. We might even say that the cloud of His presence will be with them and in them always. The Ghost is in the Cloud.

Even more, the Ghost is the Cloud.

In John 14:12 Jesus makes this astonishing statement: *"He who believes in Me, the works that I do he will do also, and greater works than these he will do, because I go to My Father."* It is a remarkable idea that the one who believes in Jesus will do greater things than He Himself did. But He says that this greater work is contingent on something. It will happen, Jesus says, *"because I go to My Father."* This is an important part, indeed, the essential part of this promise. The greater works we are called to do can only happen because Jesus goes to the Father. That is because, to again use our water metaphor, the flowing stream is being replaced by the misty cloud. The same God present in different form.

"Nevertheless I tell you the truth, it is to your advantage that I go away; for if I do not go away, the Helper will not come to you; but if I depart, I will send Him to you." (John 16:7)

When Jesus walked the earth, the *"image of the invisible God"* was in a person, Jesus, in one place at one time. He was limited to a location and moved through space and time like we do. God gave Himself to the revelation of Himself through one Person. Then Jesus told the disciples that things were going to radically change. He told them that He would still be with them but those of the world would not see Him. He would go to the Father and His Ghost — a Spirit-being without a body — would embody and rest *in each of them*! *"If that same Ghost that raised Christ from the dead lives in you, He shall make your mortal bodies alive."* The Ghost of God — a spirit without a body — would be embodied in each one who abides in God. This is such an amazing and rich promise! There is so much in it, and it is only possible because Jesus left them and went to the Father. And it is precisely why those who believe will do greater things. Holy Father, Holy Son, Holy Ghost, present as One everywhere around the world, resting in the lives of those who abide in Him. In more people, in more places — greater works.

In John 16 Jesus tells the disciples that the Ghost had been with them but would soon be *in* them. In verse 16 Jesus tells them *"A little while and you will not see Me; and again a little while, and you will see Me, because I go to My Father."* The disciples said (loosely translated) "Huh?! What does *that* mean?!" He tells them that He will see them again and their weeping will turn to a joy that no one can take away. Then in verse 25 Jesus says *"... I have spoken to you in figurative language, but the time is coming when... I will tell you plainly about the Father."* Remember, Jesus is on His way to the cross in a matter of hours. When will that time be that He will see them again and will tell them plainly about the Father? He is referring to His Ghost coming to them and leading them into all truth. Jesus and His Ghost are One.

When you read John chapters 14-17 in the light of Jesus preparing the *Alongsiders* for life after the Ascension, preparing them for life with His Ghost rather than God in one body, the things He said fall into place in a much clearer way. He is not talking about the afterlife or eternity or the mansions on streets of gold. He is preparing them for the One God — the *I AM* — to make His *mone* with them in their present moment, wherever they are in the world. Likewise, He extends this privilege beyond the first believers to us and all His people everywhere in every age — to meet us and be in us in our present moment. He will no longer be confined to a body, in one place at one time. Now, He — *His Ghost* — will be with each and every one of us who abide in Him. His language naturally becomes more oblique because He speaks about a relationship between visible and invisible realms and beings, touching both heaven-life and earth-life.

"that they all may be one, as You, Father, are in Me, and I in You; that they also may be one in Us." (17:21)

"I in them, and You in Me..." (17:23)

"Father, I desire that they also whom You gave Me may be with Me where I am..." (17:24)

"... that the love with which You loved Me may be in them, and I in them." (17:26)

It is so very important that we see Jesus and His Ghost as One so that we understand that we are living *with* Him — now, in this moment — not merely living by the example of His earthly time in the body. He will not leave us as orphans. He is with us. The *mone* is important, the abiding in Him is important, the knowing is important, because the relationship and presence of the Living God is everything. This is your calling — to live with Him, glorify Him and enjoy Him forever.

Now.

Chapter 10

In the late 70s I was speaking at a youth snow retreat at Lake Tahoe. My brother-in-law went with me and we decided to try to ski. I had never skied. Jeff had done it perhaps once as a child. We headed off to what Jeff told me was the beginner slope and got on the lift. When we got off and looked down the mountain it seemed to me more like a cliff than a slope. I crept slowly across the face of the run several times, criss-crossing it in a bid to keep my speed down and my skis under me but, in one last, glorious burst I pointed my skis down the hill and took off. I knew how to go but I had no idea how to stop. As I raced toward the kids area — a corral with a wooden rail fence — I did the only thing I could think of and simply laid down, spinning across the face of the snow and sliding under the fence right into the kids corral. A guy leaning on the fence said "Well, that's *one* way to stop!" I was determined to get back up and prove to myself that I could actually ski.

We got back on the lift, went up again and I repeated this same thing several times before giving up. I told Jeff that I was done. I was obviously not meant for skiing if I could not even conquer the beginner slope.

On our way back to the lodge we were passing other skiers on their way to the lifts. Just as one group approached us a woman in the group pointed to the hill we had just been on and said loudly *"Beginner slope?! That's not the beginner slope, that's an advanced slope!"* I stopped. *"Jeff, if that's an advanced slope then maybe there's hope for me!"* We checked the trail map and found a true beginner run and did fine on it. We skied the rest of the day and had a great time together, and I got my confidence back.

What does the voice of God sound like? Do you think it could sound like that woman we passed?

We had a Persian cat named Milo that we inadvertently poisoned by using the wrong kind of flea medicine on her. She was convulsing and growing weaker by the moment. We called the vet who immediately referred us to the animal hospital at UC, Davis, about an hour away. We called and they told us to get there as quickly as we could as our cat would probably need intravenous and digestive tract infusions. They also told us how expensive this was going to be. We were shocked and weren't sure if we wanted to spend that much, but we went anyway. At a stop light while we were discussing whether we should spend the money to do this my eyes fell on the back of a large white Cadillac in the next lane. I could see most of the license plate, and it said "IV MILO." *IV MILO!* I pointed it out to Cindy and told her we were moving ahead with this care for Milo. When the car pulled away we saw the rest of the license plate — IV MILOV — meaning For My Love, I suppose. But what it meant to me was different. As it turned out, the crew at the hospital grew to love Milo so much that they did much more than called for and charged us nearly nothing for it.

So, again I ask what does the voice of God sound like? Could it be in the letters of a license plate? Could it be in a passing remark by a stranger?

When God speaks, His words become things — stars, planets, mountains, animals, miracles. Remember, *Words Make Things*. The voice of God doesn't always come to us in audible form. In fact, I think it's rather rare that it does. Instead, God often speaks to us through the things we can see and hear around us, through the things His words made.

This is my Father's world
And to my listening ears
All nature sings and round me rings
The music of the spheres

The servant of Moses, sent out to find a wife for Moses' son, stumbled upon her by happenstance and said of it *"being on the way, the Lord led me."* It was his own decision to stop at the well outside the city of Nahor at that precise time that brought him into contact with the young lady.

The Eastern magicians/scholars/astrologers read in the heavens the coming of the Messiah and confidently left their homes, following the guidance of the star that led them to Bethlehem. God spoke to them in the night time sky.

You probably have a similar story of God leading you through what has been called the "dark sayings of God." (Ps. 78:2) It can be a song on the radio, a seeming random comment, a thought in your own mind, a license plate or even what might look like merely a minor inconvenience. One friend told me that he and his wife both had the front headlights on their new cars go out at the same time. He felt that God was speaking to them about their future direction. He moves in mysterious ways. His words make things and He uses those things, expressions of His imagination, to 'speak' to us. This underscores the importance of that little phrase in Hebrews we discussed earlier — *"by the word of."* Look around you. Everything you can see is an expression of the imagination of God created through His Word. Anything and everything you sense or perceive has the potential to be God's voice to you. *"He that has ears to hear, let him hear."*

One of the foundational patterns of the universe is rhythm. Everything is rhythm. We call it frequency or oscillation sometimes but a frequency and oscillation are still a rhythm. I have been producing music for several decades. I had my own studio and was privileged to record many wonderful artists and albums. One of the first things that must be done when preparing to record a song is to establish the BPM — beats per minute — and to lay that out as the undergirding framework of the recording process. The song needs the proper rhythm or frequency to make it the best it could be. We started in the 70s with click tracks by simply recording a metronome.

When digital recording became the norm it was very exciting to me because we could easily set the BPM in the recording software and change it until we got what we wanted. We could also see the audio waves we recorded represented on our computer screens. We could look at the rhythm of a single wave pattern. But everything we can see, hear, taste, touch and smell is exciting our senses through rhythm. Bodies keep rhythm. Your heart does, too. So do planets as they spin in one rhythm and revolve in another. Sound is measured in waves, or frequencies, and so is light. In fact, both sound and light can be measured at different points on the same scale. Your eyes and ears are both sensing the same thing— rhythmic oscillations, waves— only at different frequencies!

I read recently about Royal Rife, an inventor that discovered in the 1930s that what he called the "mortal oscillatory rate" of pathogens were each unique. In other words, each pathogen had its own rhythm. He claimed to be able to destroy them without disturbing the body they were in by blasting them with vibrations in the same unique frequency. Whether his claims were sound or not, the discovery that things have unique rhythms is intriguing.

The Word that created everything was not written. It was spoken by a living being. It reverberated through the universe, once high and then low, sometimes deep and sometimes shimmering, at times very loud and at other times nearly imperceptible. The Word was making things and with each different sound and rhythm came a sun, a planet, an ocean, a mountain, a plant, an animal and, finally, a man and a woman.

The man and woman became a race and we learned to measure the rhythms of the universe around us and to move with these rhythms though the seconds that make a minute, the minutes that make an hour, the hours that make a day, that become a week and that make a year. Humans tripped their way through the decades of their lives, moving, as Eugene Peterson said, in the "unforced rhythms of grace."

Through all of this God is calling you to dance with Him in His rhythm. Life is not wrestling, but romance. He calls us to surrender all. But what does surrender look like? For some they can only imagine lying on the floor and waiting for God to pick them up and move them like a marionette. In their minds they are not moving, they are being moved. But what God wants is the kind of surrender that moves *with* Him through the moments and days of a lifetime, like a partner being guided by an expert dancer.

Our surrender is not to give up and lie down but to stop countering His moves and, instead, to move with Him. We spend so much time wrestling with God. We don't seem to trust Him enough to move with Him. We put our defenses up because we think we have a better idea for ourselves than He does. We're frightened of the unknown, perhaps. Or maybe we think we won't be able to keep up. My daughter-in-law was unexpectedly whisked out onto the dance floor at a wedding. The man who swept her up was a confident, experienced dancer who knew how to lead with one hand in hers and the other hand in the small of her back. She came off the floor joyful and confident. She felt like a real dancer! His guidance was so good that all she needed to do was follow his little nudges and she glided effortlessly through the dance.

This is what God wants for you!

He will guide you perfectly through the rhythms of your life.

CHAPTER 11

"If it was working, our churches would be full."

A friend said this to me just before the service in her church when I told her I was going to speak about my lack of enthusiasm for the present state of American Christianity. Nearly every American church I have been in, with several notable exceptions, have fewer people in them now than they did ten years, or even five years, ago. It would be easy and comfortable to blame this on the devil, resisting us, stymieing our best efforts, conspiring with the prevailing wicked political and moral culture against us. It's not our fault if it's the devil's fault, right? However, we don't see the early Christians retreating and hiding away in their gatherings, letting themselves off the hook because evil Rome was against them. We don't see that because it didn't happen.

Rather, my impression is that we are like the emperor with his new clothes that are really no clothes at all. We're prancing around as though we are clothed in fine spiritual garb when we are naked. We sing and shout about how great our God is and yet live just like the culture around us — no power; no abundance to our lives; nothing pressed down, shaken together or running over. Someone has to laugh and point it out, and the world around us has obligingly done so — *the Emperor has no clothes!*

Sunday services in churches across the country seem like so many little plays. We know our parts. Someone on the platform says something really good about God and we say "Amen!" We proclaim that our God is awesome and all powerful and yet nothing dynamic or explosive happens among us. Our pastors give us "principles for practical living," "habits worth having," teaching us to be more and more and more *like* Jesus. Discipleship becomes a class you can take, information you ingest, and a course of study with a Q&A, a test and a measurable goal.

We sing worship songs that often have no resonance with our own lives. I remember once we were singing a good song that said they — the non-Christian onlookers who convert — would "dance with joy like we're dancing now." I looked at the audience and saw that no one was dancing. I thought ruefully to myself that they were probably singing the truth: whoever joins them in their party won't be dancing, either.

What is wrong with us?! How did we decide to play the part of good Christians without having any of the dynamic energy that comes from living in moment by moment relationship with the Creator of the universe?! When did we decide it was acceptable to talk about the power of God without ever having to demonstrate or experience it?!

Have you ever seen anyone raised from death back to life? I have. Have you seen anyone healed of a terminal cancer? I have. Have you seen a young freak high on mescaline delivered instantly from his addiction, speaking in a new language of prayer and called into a lifetime of passionate ministry? I have. Have you seen a young girl who, between the ages of eight and twelve, was abused by a priest so many times she can't count them; whose life was so transformed by the power of God that she was truly dancing in His love? I know that girl. She married and raised wonderful children and loves God so much for the change He made in her. I love Him for it, too.

I am asking if you have seen these things but what I'm really asking is *why have you not seen these things?* Our churches have become safe, our services sterile. The excitement in our churches is faux-dangerous, like Disneyland. Every Sunday morning we get in, buckle up and go swooping up and around, dangling over the abyss, careening around corners and, finally, rolling back into the station, breathless and excited perhaps, but always safe, knowing full well that we were never for a moment in any real danger.

Is this living?!

Is this all there is to being fully alive?!

We are people-pleasers. More than anything, we say, we want new people to come to our churches. After all, this is the Great Commission, isn't it? We want it so much that we dare not do anything that might offend or confuse them. We advertise that in our churches you won't be made to feel uncomfortable. *When did God ever guarantee that we wouldn't be uncomfortable?!* We change our language to be warm and inclusive and less judgmental. Let there be no more talk of sin or guilt. Remove words like sanctification, justification, righteousness or propitiation. Drop that harsh, off-putting *contra mundum* idea for *cum mundi*.

Our worship songs become, in the words of a Christian music veteran, "co-dependent love songs to God."

"Baby, oh baby, oh baby" becomes "Jesus, oh Jesus, oh Jesus!" We constantly remind ourselves how precious we are, how much we are valued and the great things we can do… in His name, of course. It sometimes sounds so pathetic and needy.

One of the main problems is that Church Growth has become the "chief end of man" and is, in our opinion, our highest responsibility. We must grow God's church for Him. There is a multi-billion dollar industry to teach pastors the systems they need to attract people to their churches. Of course, the message is that you cannot possibly expect to attract people and grow your church if you don't have the right systems. It seems they don't care if they have *Jabba the Church*, however fat and useless it may be, as long as it's a BIG church. Institutions, systems, processes, principles — *skubala!*

Jesus asked the disciples who men said that He was. They told Him some of the opinions and rumors flying around. Then He asked them who *they* said He was. Peter replied that He was the Christ, the Son of the Living God. Jesus told Peter that this was revealed to him by the Father. Then He said that on this rock (of revelation) *"I WILL BUILD MY CHURCH."*

Jesus will build His church. He will build it on the revelation of Himself to those who want to see Him. He is well capable of it and He said Himself that it was His to do, not ours. The systems, the "programs for the whole family," the non-offensive language of the church, the abject and craven desire to please outsiders at all costs, are showing people one thing: the emperor has no clothes. Frankly, we're not offering people a transformed life that will affect every choice they make, we're asking them to replace Rotary or Kiwanis or golf with church attendance — or merely squeeze it into their social calendar. And all we can seem to offer them is that, if they try really hard, they might become a little more like Jesus. Phooey.

If this is what you want then go on without me. If this is what 'Christianity' is about then I can't blame so many others who used to go to church, who came there hoping for something *other* than what they already had.

They had tried and failed. They had seen the end of themselves. They knew they didn't have it in them to transform themselves and, sadly, the church just told them to try a little harder to be like Jesus. We gave them principles when they needed presence. We gave them platitudes when they needed power. We were too sensible to tell them about the Ghost in the Cloud. We wanted them to believe that they could, indeed, have clarity when we knew in our hearts that we didn't even have it ourselves. When will we admit that there is a mystery to God and to life that we must embrace to truly live? Can we make peace with the Ghost? the Cloud? the Unknowing?

Through all this, the Church lives and she is beautiful, like the bride she is. The lifeless, religious forms cannot hold her. She will — she does! — burst out into life with every small opportunity given. I long to see the Church in the glory God intended for her — as the full expression of the presence of God in the world, living moment by moment — fully alive! — with Him and in His power, loving dangerously, forgiving recklessly, rising fearlessly, dancing through the mysteries at the gentle touch of His hands, living with the Ghost in the Cloud.

Will you join Him?

Do you have anything better to do?